Original title:
A Taste of Tropical Summer

Copyright © 2025 Creative Arts Management OÜ
All rights reserved.

Author: Riley Hawthorne
ISBN HARDBACK: 978-1-80581-698-0
ISBN PAPERBACK: 978-1-80581-225-8
ISBN EBOOK: 978-1-80581-698-0

Harmony of Heat and Chill

On the beach in wild attire,
Sunglasses perched, we never tire.
Ice cream drips, a messy race,
Seagulls laugh as we lose face.

Flip-flops flying, tan lines bold,
Stories of sunburns never told.
Feeling like we're on a spree,
Laughter drowned out by the sea.

Island Echoes and Elysian Vibes.

Coconut drinks in our hands,
Making castles in the sands.
Turtles think they own the shore,
We chase them down, 'Come back for more!'

Bikinis bright, a rainbow spread,
Lost my hat, it's fled instead!
Tiki torches light the night,
Dance like no one's in our sight.

Sun-Kissed Serenity

Sipping juice, it dribbles down,
Sticky fingers all around.
We wear our sunscreen with flair,
Giggling, oh, the funny glare.

Beach volleyball, we jump and sway,
Hit the ball, it flies away!
Chasing shadows, what a show,
Watch the sun set, golden glow.

Whispering Palm Leaves

Palm trees dance with breezy thrills,
Check my drink, oh, what a spill!
Laughter echoes through the night,
Stars above, they twinkle bright.

Crabs in suits play hide and seek,
Dodging waves with tiny squeaks.
Life's a party, we all cheer,
Under the moon, we found our beer.

Hidden Isle Reverie

On a hidden isle, sun shines bright,
Coconuts in sight, a comical flight.
Laughter erupts, a dance with a crab,
Twisting and turning, oh what a blab!

Seagulls squawk high, stealing my fries,
I chase them around, much to my surprise.
Flip-flops are flying, the dog joins the fun,
Summer's a circus, oh look, here comes a bun!

With palm trees swaying like they're on stage,
A monkey throws coconuts, oh, what a rage!
Sipping on punch, no worries today,
Except for the sunburn that's here to stay.

Now the sun's setting, painted in gold,
Time for tall tales to be humorously told.
Life on this isle, a laugh on each wave,
In paradise found, we're all just a bit brave!

Colorful Tropic Tapestry

In the tropics, where colors collide,
I found a toucan who's terribly wide.
He gobbles my snacks, with glee and a flair,
Leaving just crumbs in the tropical air.

Hammocks are swinging, I jump for a ride,
But land on a turtle, oh how he sighed!
He looks up at me, with the wisest old eyes,
'Stick to the beach, kid, avoid the surprise!'

Watermelons splatter, on friends far and near,
As we battle with fruit, but we giggle in cheer.
A pineapple hat on a fellow named Pete,
He dances around, isn't he quite neat?

As twilight descends, we roar with delight,
Under stars that twinkle, oh what a sight!
With laughter and joy, we'll always remember,
The humor and fun of each sunny day's ember.

Joyful Journeys in Paradise

On a beach so bright and sunny,
A crab danced, oh so funny.
With sunglasses perched on his eyes,
He slid on sand, a big surprise!

Palms waved like they hold a joke,
A parrot squawked as it awoke.
Flip-flops flopped, a wild parade,
Each step a giggle, bright and made!

Lively Markets and Spiced Delights

In the market, colors swirl,
Mangoes twirl and pineapples whirl.
The vendors shout, what a loud cheer,
As I trip on a basket, oh dear!

Coconut juice, a slippery treat,
I spill some while dancing my beat.
With every taste, a chuckle's born,
Do I wear fruit or eat it? I'm torn!

Currents of Colorful Currents

The waves tickle my toes, oh so grand,
Beaches stretched like a long, lazy band.
Seashells laugh as I skip and slide,
A fish flops out, what a fishy ride!

Surfboards wobble, a chaotic sight,
As dolphins jump with pure delight.
In this splashy circus, I lose my hat,
And the sea claims it, just like that!

Radiant Horizons

Sunsets turn skies into confetti,
A squirrel tries to steal my spaghetti.
The stars join in, they wink and play,
As night drapes its cozy ballet!

Fireflies dance, lighting the night,
A bug in my hair gives me a fright.
With laughter echoing, we spin around,
In this bright bliss, joy knows no bound!

The Scent of Salt and Sand

Seagulls squawk with a flair,
Wearing sunglasses, they strut like a pair.
Kids chase waves, dodging the spray,
While crabs play tag in a quirky display.

Sandy toes in flip-flops, so funny,
Sunburned noses look like a honey.
Ice cream drips in the heat of the day,
Making sticky smiles in a comical way.

Sunset Bougainvillea

Bougainvillea blooms in vivid hues,
Dancing breezes bring the news.
Lizards sunbathe, striking a pose,
While a giant tortoise takes things slow.

Flip-flops flapping, laughter abounds,
As kids build castles with funny sounds.
A coconut falls with a comical thud,
It's a game of dodge in the warm summer mud.

Island Melodies

Steel drums clink with a rhythmic cheer,
While parrots squawk, "Is the rum here?"
Hula dancers twirl with a giggling twist,
In this paradise, how could you resist?

Fishermen boast of the one that got away,
While mermaids laugh at their cheesy display.
Sunshine and laughter turn the tide,
On this island, there's no place to hide.

Coconut Lime Lullaby

Coconuts bob like heads in the sea,
Limes roll away, oh-so-sneaky!
Sipping cocktails under palm tree shade,
Come join the let's-make-a-mess parade!

Tiny crabs with a waddle to show,
Dance at sunset, putting on a show.
Splashing around like a silly old cat,
Life's a beach, just imagine that!

Sun-Kissed Dreams

Sunshine spills on sandy toes,
Ice cream drips, and laughter flows.
Flip-flops dance, they know the beat,
While sunbaked seagulls seek a treat.

Coconut hats and shades so bright,
A crab in shorts gives quite a fright.
Beachballs bounce and free spirits soar,
As sunscreen slides to the ocean floor.

Whispering Palms

Palms are swaying, having a chat,
One whispers secrets to a hat.
The breeze giggles and gives a wink,
While locals argue, 'Is it a drink?'

Lemons squabble with lines of gin,
Tanning lotion's sticking to skin.
Shadows dance, but no one is scared,
Who knew being silly was so well-prepared?

Mango Murmurs

Mangoes tumble and roll away,
A fruity game of hide and play.
Dancing ants in a sticky line,
"Hey! That mango's definitely mine!"

Sliced and juicy, a spectacular mess,
Who knew fruit could wear such stress?
With sticky fingers and giggles galore,
Mango parties leave you begging for more.

Salty Breeze Serenade

Waves come crashing, surfboards fly,
Seagulls swoop, oh how they cry!
A dog in shades, a pirate's delight,
Chasing after a kite in flight.

Salty whispers from the sea,
"Watch your step, don't trip on me!"
But trippers laugh, they soar and glide,
In this wild, salty, summer ride.

Sunlit Soiree

The sun is bright, a golden glow,
It makes the ice cream melt so slow.
The beach balls bounce, oh what a sight,
While seagulls squawk, taking their flight.

We dance in sand, all toes exposed,
With goofy moves, we've surely dozed.
Laughter erupts, like waves at shore,
Who knew fun could be such a chore?

Sipping drinks with funny straws,
Each sip brings giggles, applause and wow!
Under the sun, we eat too much,
Who knew coconuts had such a touch?

As evening falls, we sing a tune,
While burned toasts soar like a balloon.
With marshmallows stuck on every face,
We'll remember this wild, tasty race!

The Dance of Dandelions

Dandelions sway in cheerful glee,
Whispering secrets to a buzzing bee.
With silly hats and leaping feet,
We pirouette to summer's beat.

A breeze blows through with tickling grace,
As we chase shadows in a wild race.
The day grows old but we won't quit,
Just one more dance, we can't just sit!

Confetti flies from grassy knolls,
Our laughter juggles with seagull strolls.
Each twist and turn, a friend to twirl,
In this crazy world, we laugh and whirl.

As petals fall in twilight's glow,
Our giggles echo, soft and low.
With dandelions flying high and free,
We'll dream of more fun, just you and me!

Floating on Fruity Clouds

Fluffy clouds made of cotton wool,
Drift through skies, oh ain't that cool?
With fruity flavors, we take a ride,
Banana boats on a berry tide.

Pineapple hats and mango dance,
We twirl and tumble, given the chance.
Watermelon smiles, chocolate skies,
When summer's here, no one denies!

Sipping smoothies that spin and whirl,
Each fruity sip gives my heart a twirl.
As mangoes glisten and berries gleam,
We float on flavors, living the dream!

But when the sun pulls on our chains,
And laughter ebbs like summer rains,
We'll hug our clouds and take a bow,
For fruity fun is here right now!

Island Whispers

On sandy shores, where whispers play,
The coconuts laugh at the crabs today.
With flip-flops flapping, we roam around,
Finding treasures where fun is found.

The surfboards giggle on waves so blue,
As we dive headfirst, with skies so true.
Each splash brings shouts of sheer delight,
Turning the beach into a wild sight.

Palm trees sway, in a fanciful dance,
With sunburned noses, we take a chance.
Chasing sunsets, we paint the sky,
Who knew island life could fly so high?

As night creeps in with a starlit gleam,
We'll toast to laughter and share a dream.
For island whispers, secrets to share,
Hold the joy of summer in salty air!

Sunkissed Reflections

Sunshine spills like lemonade,
Belly flops and cannonballs made.
Flip-flops flying, fashion galore,
Sunscreen smears, a sticky rapport.

Coconuts laugh with faces so round,
While sandy toes wiggle, lost, and found.
Seagulls squawk, a comical show,
Sandcastles tumble, oh no, oh no!

Palm trees dance in the sultry breeze,
While mischief hides among the leaves.
Flip-flops squeak on the boardwalk's way,
Summer clumsiness on full display!

Laughter echoes, the day takes the stage,
Joking with sunburns, we age like sage.
In this bliss, we're all misfit toys,
Catching rays with our foolish joys.

Tropical Twilight Tales

Under stars like scattered seeds,
We gather tales and coconut deeds.
A parrot steals a snack with flair,
While crabs march off without a care.

Laughter drips like melting ice,
As we share stories, not so nice.
Naps on hammocks, swaying slow,
Then kaboom! The mangoes blow!

Fireflies join our evening dance,
While we attempt a limbo chance.
Checkered blankets, snacks galore,
Oops! I dropped my chips, what a score!

In this twilight, we howl and sing,
With overstated pride, we do our thing.
Where fun meets awkwardness, we thrive,
Under the moon, we feel alive!

Lagoon Light and Shadows

Reflections skip on water's skin,
Where kooky ducks try to swim.
Laughter echoes from the shore,
An ice cream cone, not one, but four!

Sun hats slide, and goggles pinch,
While waves give us a gentle inch.
Sunscreen wars on a friend's back,
A sticky prank in the midday snack.

Fishing rods twist in a tangle mess,
Each catch is just a feathered guess.
Lizards leap with acrobat flair,
While we find snacks hidden with care.

Evening brings a golden show,
As crickets chirp the summer flow.
Amidst the shadows, we laugh and cheer,
Lagoon life, oh dear, oh dear!

Marigold Mornings

Mornings burst like citrus surprise,
With mischief hiding in sunlit eyes.
Breakfast dances on plates with glee,
Sticky fingers, just like honey bee!

Pancakes flip and syrup spills,
As kids make their own wacky thrills.
Jumping jacks in pajamas bright,
While sunshine sneaks in, oh what a sight!

A parade of kids rushes outside,
With sea shells found in sandals wide.
Splashing puddles turn into fun,
Funniest morning under the sun!

As flowers bloom with grand acclaim,
We giggle and play, refusing to tame.
A marigold dawn, a riotous scene,
In our hearts, we're always serene!

Mango Skies at Dusk

Mangoes tumble from the trees,
As I catch them with such ease.
Sticky fingers, laughs galore,
Who knew fruit could fill with score?

Squirrel steals my ripe delight,
Leaping off—what a sight!
I chase him, what a farce,
Running barefoot, like a star!

Sunset paints the skies with gold,
Stories of the summer told.
With sunsets bright and skies ablaze,
You'd think I was in a daze!

Mango cheeks and silly grins,
Who knew joy was full of spins?
This summer's flair in every bite,
Mango dreams take off in flight!

Ocean Breeze Ballet

Waves dance like they're at a ball,
Pirouetting, oh, how they sprawl!
Crabs in tuxedos steal the show,
As seagulls provide a rowdy blow!

Flip-flops flop, I trip and fall,
At the beach, I seek beach ball.
But it rolls away with glee,
I chase it, oh, the sight of me!

Children giggle, sand in hair,
Build a castle, but beware!
For the tide, it comes alive,
And swallows my home—oh, I thrive!

Sun-kissed skin, and salty hair,
Ocean breeze, without a care.
Laughter echoes 'round the shore,
In this ballet, who wants more?

Hibiscus Dreams and Rhythms

Hibiscus blooms in pretty hues,
Trying on its jazzy shoes.
Bumblebees for dance invade,
In this flower parade, they played!

Rhythms pulse in vibrant air,
While I twirl without a care.
Tripped on roots, down I go,
A laughing flower steals the show!

Scent of petals fills the breeze,
Tickling noses, with such ease.
My dance goes wild, so unrefined,
Even butterflies are maligned!

With petals in my tangled hair,
I sashay here, I twirl with flair.
In hibiscus dreams I find,
Summer laughter intertwined!

Laughter on the Lava Rocks

Lava rocks beneath my feet,
Tumble down, a silly feat.
I slip and slide, a playful dance,
The universe gives me a chance!

Hotter than a summer's day,
I wonder if I'll find my way.
Magma's warmth, the sun's my pal,
But watch your step—the rocks can yell!

Sunburnt noses, giggles loud,
A balancing act, I feel so proud.
Each step's a test, a challenge grand,
As I wander this volcanic land.

With laughter echoing in the air,
My summer quest has flair to spare.
These lava rocks, unpredictable spree,
Who knew nature's playground could be so free?

Driftwood and Sun Rays

Driftwood on the shore, it grins,
Telling tales of fishy sins.
Sun rays tickle sandy toes,
While crabs dance in tidy rows.

Flip-flops fly in playful glee,
As seagulls steal our lunch, oh me!
A beach ball bounces out of sight,
Leaving us in a giggling fight.

Sunscreen smears, a slippery mess,
We slide around in summer's dress.
A piña colada, sweet and cold,
Cheers to stories yet untold.

So here's to sand, and laughter's flair,
To driftwood dreams beyond compare.
With sun-kissed cheeks and silly dances,
Let's embrace these light-hearted prances.

Jewel-Toned Journeys

In water so clear, the fish wear crowns,
Dancing like they own the towns.
Shells are treasures, colors so bright,
An oyster's wink brings pure delight.

Mango smoothies, sips of gold,
The blender roars, the kitchen's bold!
Chasing rainbows, a slippery show,
Watch out now, the waves might throw!

Flip-flops squawk, they have their say,
As we twirl and spin in public display.
A coconut shell hobbles on by,
Pretending to be a shifty spy.

So let's embark on journeys chaste,
Through jewel-toned waters, life embraced.
With laughter, splashes, a runaway kite,
We'll dance through days and party all night.

Celestial Waters

Under skies as blue as pie,
Water's whisper makes us sigh.
Ducks in shades, they strut on by,
Wearing sunglasses, oh my, oh my!

A snorkeling mask makes quite a sight,
Flippers flopping left and right.
While mermaids giggle, tails all gleam,
Creating quite the underwater dream.

Hammocks sway, a balmy breeze,
With all our snacks, oh dear, oh please!
Sandwiches fly like frisbees bold,
While seagulls laugh at our lunch grown cold.

So dip your toes and feel the fun,
Celestial waters, where we run.
With giggles loud and spirits high,
Let's splash in rhythm, you and I.

Swaying to the Samba

Under the palms, we shimmy and shake,
Our moves are wild, make no mistake!
With coconuts clinking, we twirl around,
To samba beats, we're spellbound.

Tropical drinks in hand, oh yes,
But spilled it seems, we wear our mess.
The dance floor's hot; our feet can't rest,
A limbo pole? We're not the best!

Towels fly like capes in flight,
As we dive in the cool moonlight.
Flip-flops twirl in samba bliss,
With funny moments, can't be amiss.

So come, and join this cheerful groove,
Let laughter guide, let's make our move.
With sun-kissed smiles and hearts so free,
We'll sway and laugh in joyful glee.

Tropical Tides and Treasures

The coconut danced with the sea,
A flip-flop fell off, oh me!
Sand stuck to my toes like glue,
Is there a towel? I'd like one too!

Crabs bring snacks on their little claws,
Eating them quickly would cause some flaws.
The waves giggle, what a silly sound,
And jellyfish play hide and seek all around.

Pineapples wearing shades, so grand,
A beach ball rolling—nobody planned!
Sunburns and laughter mingle in air,
As sunscreen bottles vanish in the glare.

Seagulls squawk jokes, they think they're wise,
Throw breadcrumbs? Watch them argue and rise!
Drifting on floats, we float far and wide,
In this paradise, there's no need to hide.

Sipping Sunshine

Lemonade rivers flow down the street,
Ice cubes splashing—a summer treat!
Straws wearing shades, chilling in glass,
Slurping and laughing, what a wild class!

Mangoes gossip, juicy and bright,
Whispering secrets under sunlight.
Pineapple hats on rascally kids,
Who knew fruit could start such great bids?

Coconuts wobble like they're in glee,
Caught in a race, one spills on me!
Beverages bubble, a fizzy parade,
In this carnival, worries do fade.

Cheers with confetti made out of zest,
The flavors compete for the very best,
Under the sun, laughter takes flight,
Sipping sunshine, what a pure delight!

Breeze Through the Banyan

A breeze whispers sweetly through the leaves,
Tails of kites tangled in playful weaves.
Look at that monkey, it's dancing away,
While squirrels join in for a cheeky ballet!

Fruits hang low, pretending to play,
But one sneaky rambutan rolls away.
The banyan chuckles from its leafy throne,
As bees buzz near with a silly drone.

Kids chase shadows in the gentle sway,
Jumping on grass, making their own way.
The breeze spins stories, tales of the sun,
While laughter rings out, oh, what a fun run!

Picnics laid out, sandwiches flop,
A jar of pickles that just wouldn't stop.
In the embrace of trees, all fears dissolve,
Where nature and laughter quickly evolve.

Vibrant Hues of Hibiscus

Hibiscus blooms with a grin so wide,
Colors like confetti, they can't hide.
Dancing in gardens, a floral parade,
Spilling their secrets, bold and unafraid.

Bees in pajamas, buzzing all day,
Sipping sweet nectar, come join the fray!
A butterfly sneezes, it flutters, oh dear!
The flowers giggle, there's nothing to fear.

Grasshoppers hopping, a comical crew,
They dance through petals, who knew they could brew?
Swirling and twirling, their leaps are so grand,
In this riot of color, all nonsense is planned.

Under the sun, the colors collide,
A rainbow of laughter, nowhere to hide.
In the bloom of summer, the fun's always near,
With vibrant hues brightening up the cheer!

Exotic Fruits and Gentle Mists

In the jungle, fruits hang low,
Bananas dance and mangoes glow.
Pineapples giggle, all in a heap,
While coconuts snore, taking a nap, so deep.

Papayas whisper secrets, oh so sweet,
While lychees laugh and shuffle their feet.
The dragon fruit dons a silly hat,
Saying, "Try me first!" like a chubby cat.

Limes roll over, making a mess,
While cherries tease, "We're the best, no less!"
Kiwis wear sunglasses, strutting their stuff,
The tropical party just can't get enough!

Grapefruits giggle, "We're a little tart,"
While rambutan pleads, "Please take heart!"
In this fruity fiesta, oh what a scene,
Mirthful melon bursts with spontaneous glee!

Barefoot on Warm Shores

Barefoot we wander on golden sands,
Dodging crabs with tiny hands.
Seagulls squawk like they're telling tales,
As the ocean dances and gently exhales.

Flip-flops flung, and laughter erupts,
Shells like treasures, picked up in scoops.
Sandcastles built that look like blobs,
While waves crash in like giggling mobs.

Sunburned noses, red as a beet,
Chasing waves with silly little feet.
"Can't catch me!" we shout and squeal,
As the sea tricks us with a slippery deal.

Drifting high on a breeze so fine,
We pretend to fly like a bird divine.
With friends beside and sunset's glow,
These funny summer days are the best, you know!

Sunset Sips and Sweet Memories

Sipping cocktails with tiny umbrellas,
As laughter dances with the jovial fellas.
Strawberry splashes make a splashy sound,
While lime wedges climb all around.

The sun dips low, turning purple and pink,
As we toast with laughter and clink, clink, clink.
In this paradise, we feel so witty,
With sips so sweet, oh what a pity!

Pineapple straws and coconut bowls,
Mixing our potions to cheer our souls.
"I'm the mojito king!" someone will claim,
While the piña coladas cry out, "What a game!"

Even the sunset craves our delight,
As we giggle about the silly sights.
Sweet memories formed with each playful sip,
In this zany haven, we happily slip.

Lullabies of the Island Breeze

The island hums a cheeky tune,
As palm trees sway beneath the moon.
Coconut crabs play hopscotch nightly,
While sea turtles glide on breezes lightly.

Fireflies prance with their little glow,
Whispering tales only the stars know.
"Did you see that splash?" one raccoon yells,
As the fish reply, "We enjoy our shells!"

The hammock sways with a gentle chuckle,
As the night air tickles and begins to cuddle.
"Dare to dream?" the moon lightheartedly beams,
While the ocean murmurs our wildest dreams.

Frogs croak jokes and crickets sing,
In this funny land of giggling bling.
Though lullabies drift softly with poise,
The heart of the island bursts with noise!

Citrus Glow at Daybreak

Morning spills its tangy cheer,
Lemons dance like they have no fear.
Oranges giggle, plump and round,
While limes roll on the sandy ground.

In a world where fruits conspire,
A grapefruit wears a hat of fire.
Mangoes strut, a juicy parade,
With pineapple shades, they won't be swayed.

Chasing sunbeams, they leap and spin,
Cracking jokes, let the fun begin!
Sipping sunshine from a coconut,
The laughter echoes, it's never shut.

A Symphony of Coconuts

Coconuts play a bouncy tune,
Tapping rhythms under the moon.
They roll and tumble, what a sight,
Each one dreams of a dizzy flight.

Bananas laugh, they join the jam,
Swinging gently on a leafy tram.
Pineapples flip, with perfect flair,
While coconuts tease with salty air.

A conga line of fruits all sway,
In the breeze, they sing and play.
With every plop upon the sand,
These fruity antics are just grand!

Seashells and Sunshine

Seashells giggle in the sun,
As waves crash in, oh what fun!
A crab joins in with a silly dance,
While starfish laugh in a sunlit trance.

Sandy toes and fruity treats,
Chasing seagulls with happy beats.
Watermelons in the shade recline,
With jokes so ripe, they're quite divine.

Orange sunsets spill their bliss,
All the world shares a fruity kiss.
Seashells sing, both loud and clear,
As sunshine fades, their joys adhere.

Fruit-Filled Serenade

Underneath a mango tree,
Fruits unite for a melody.
Strawberries serenade the breeze,
While cherries sway with utmost ease.

Peaches chuckle, soft and sweet,
Jiving along to a drumline beat.
Pears roll over, bursting with fun,
As grapes bounce like they've just won.

A fruit parade in vibrant hues,
With laughter bright and quirky views.
Bananas split in a comic show,
While melons giggle in a row.

Paradise Found

In flip-flops I roam, all sandy and free,
Where the sun sings a tune just for me.
The seagulls squawk tunes like jazz on the breeze,
While I chase after ice cream, oh, where's my knees?

Palm trees are dancing, it's quite the display,
A coconut falls, and I jump out of the way.
My drink's got a tiny umbrella hat,
I sip with finesse, while the bugs love to chat.

Beach balls are bouncing, kids scatter about,
Trying to catch laughter, or toss it out.
Sandcastles are rising, oh, what a sight,
Until a wave crashes, oh what a fright!

So here I relax, with a burrito to munch,
With laughter and quirks, oh, what a fun bunch!
The sun starts to set, painting skies like a flame,
In this paradise found, there's no room for shame.

Prismatic Rainbows in the Sky

Umbrella drinks swirling with hues bright as noon,
I swear I just saw a three-legged raccoon!
The clouds wear pink hats, and the sun is a clown,
While rainbows play hopscotch, while I settle down.

Parrots are squawking some newer slang phrase,
I nod like I get it, in a sun-drenched haze.
Flip-flops are squeaking a quirky old tune,
As I twirl with my coconut like a fun cartoon.

Watermelon slices drip juice down my chin,
I laugh at my life, oh, what a win!
The waves toss confetti, or is that just foam?
Either way, it feels like a carnival home.

So on this fine afternoon, with laughter so spry,
Let's dance like the waves, and reach for the sky.
For every giggle counts, 'neath this luminous glow,
In this whimsical place where the funny things flow!

Castaway Serenade

Stranded on this isle, with a smile on my face,
I'm the king of coconuts, oh! What a place!
A crab tries to dance, but he's got two left feet,
While I join in with moves that can't be beat.

The sun sets with flair, in hues of wild cheer,
I mistake a dolphin for my long-lost dear.
Banana peels slip through my amusing plight,
As I sing to the stars in the cool of the night.

The island's my stage with a beach for my floor,
I imagine the audience calling for more.
Seashells are clapping, or maybe it's me,
Making friends with the waves while sipping iced tea.

So here I shall stay, with my pirate-like grin,
In this castaway world, where the fun begins.
As I sway to the rhythm, my spirit runs free,
In a serenade of joy, for the world to see.

Cocooned in Coconut

Coconuts rolling, oh what a scene,
With monkeys factorial, being quite mean.
I joined in their game, but they laughed, oh dear,
Now I'm dodging their laughter, with coconut fear.

Sipping from halved shells, it tastes like a dream,
While my floaty's a whale, yes, made from ice cream!
I take a big bite; it's a slippery feat,
And land with a splash—oh joy, can't be beat!

The sun in the sky shares its playful grin,
While I juggle pineapples; oh where do I begin?
The breeze whispers secrets that tickle my toes,
As I dance with a crab in a coconut pose.

So here in my fortress, of laughter and sun,
Life's a zany circus, oh, isn't it fun?
In this tropical cocoon, I feel so alive,
With giggles and mischief, watch my spirit thrive!

A Symphony of Scents

Mango in the air, oh what a delight,
Laughter floats around, day turns to night.
Coconuts are clapping, palms sway with glee,
Even the old flip-flops dance in the spree.

Scent of sunscreen mingles, it's quite a show,
Seagulls cackle loudly, stealing the glow.
Pineapple's singing, calling friends near,
Nothing like this to bring out the cheer!

Banana peels slipping, a comedic scene,
Watch out for the beach ball, oh it's quite mean!
Sun-kissed and giggling, we embrace the fun,
In this tropical dream, laughter's never done.

Crab walks in style, with swagger and flair,
Jellyfish jiggles, we can only stare.
With every wave crashing, a chuckle at hand,
Summer's wild ballet, oh isn't it grand!

Sunlit Journeys

The sun rockets up, ready to play,
Swimming shorts fight with sand all day.
My ice cream's melting, I chase it with speed,
It's a race with the sun, oh yes indeed!

Barefoot wanderings, toes in the sand,
I trip over nothing, well isn't that grand?
Hammock's a vessel, I'm sailing away,
Dreaming of monkeys who join in the fray.

Rum drinks are slurped, with umbrellas so bright,
A crab steals my snacks, what a funny sight!
Beach balls collide, like ships lost at sea,
Yet, somehow we're still happy and free.

Sunscreen's a puzzle, I doubt I'll escape,
With each awkward squirt, I slip into shape.
Oh summer, you joker, with so much to bring,
In these days of sunshine, our laughter will sing!

Melodies of a Coastal Day

Shells whisper secrets, the tides want to share,
While dolphins pop up, with flair and a dare.
A hula hoop's spinning, oh what a delight,
While tourists keep tripping, what a funny sight!

The beach ball's a comet, soaring so high,
Playa's the stage where all seagulls fly.
Drums made of coconuts beat out a tune,
As I try to dance but confuse the monsoon.

Swaying to rhythms, life matches the breeze,
While sunscreen's a villain, now I'm feeling wheezy.
Bikinis in camouflage, watch out for the sun,
In this festival of laughter, we all have such fun.

Crabs in tuxedos, strut past on parade,
Each one with a swagger, no fear, they invade.
The ocean's a stage for our sideways ballet,
Where every day's sunset ends in a play!

Bounty of the Bounty

Juicy fruit falls, splatters in glee,
Pineapples giggle, safe in their spree.
Fishes are swimming, choreographed styles,
While I wrestle with snacks, yielding a few smiles.

Sandwiches singing, sandwiches prancing,
As they slide off the table, oh, what a romancing!
Coconut drinks beckon, but spills are the trend,
In this circus of flavors, laughter's our friend.

The sun's casting shadows, dancing with grace,
I dance with a crab, and we both laugh in place.
Beverages spill in a curious route,
In this banquet of blunders, there's never a drought!

Juggling my mindset with fruits in the air,
I might wear a watermelon if that's fair.
All under the skies of this sunny beach spree,
A feast of hilarious, come laugh along with me!

Hibiscus Harmony

In the garden blooms a flower bright,
Hibiscus giggles in the sun's light.
Swatting bees with dance and flair,
They buzz back laughing, without a care.

Lemonade spills on sandy feet,
Laughter bubbles, oh-so-sweet.
The parrot squawks his silly song,
Join in the fun, you can't go wrong.

Palm trees sway with a playful tease,
They flitter about in the warm breeze.
Waves crash, then retreat with glee,
Chasing seashells, come play with me.

Nighttime falls, the stars take stage,
The crickets chirp, a noisy page.
Flip-flop fashion leads the way,
Dancing with shadows until the day.

The Scent of Ocean Flowers

Ocean breeze, a heavy perfume,
Where seaweed dances, a quirky bloom.
Sunglasses perched on a nose so red,
Smelling like kelp, where the sea turtles tread.

Seagulls chime in with raucous laughter,
Searching for fries but finding disaster.
Sandcastles crumble, but who really cares?
A squishy rivalry with tossed beach chairs.

A crab in a hat struts by with pride,
Challenging friends to a crustacean ride.
Salty snacks and beach ball fights,
Chasing the sunset into the night.

Under the moon, with giggles galore,
We spin like whirlpools, begging for more.
Tidal waves crash with a joyful cheer,
Ocean flowers bloom, summer is here!

Golden Sands and Laughter

Golden sands stretch, a sunlit spree,
Footprints dancing, wild and free.
Sandy sandwiches, who needs bread?
Grab a flip-flop, and give it a tread.

Beach volleyball turns to a mess,
Tangled nets and a little stress.
Someone tripped on a runaway dog,
Laughter erupts along with the fog.

Ice cream cones melt in the heat,
Sticky fingers, oh what a treat!
Seashells giggle as they pout,
Finders keepers, let's not shout!

Twilight paints the skies so bright,
Stars peek in, a merry sight.
Golden laughter fills the air,
In these moments, we shed our cares.

Tropical Sunlight's Embrace

Sunshine tickles, a warm embrace,
We dash for shade, a daring race.
Juicy fruits drip on our chins,
Messy bites lead to silly grins.

Coconuts swaying, what a sight,
A battle ensues, who'll win the fight?
With hammer and laughter, we swing away,
Cracking jokes like we crack the fray.

Flip-flops slapping on the sand,
Dancing to tunes, so unplanned.
Lime on the rim of a cool cold drink,
The secrets we share, more than we think.

As the sun sets, colors ignite,
Fireflies dance with sheer delight.
We laugh and twirl till the stars appear,
Embracing joy, summer is here!

Sunset Chimes

The sun dips low, a canvas bright,
Kids chase shadows, what a sight!
Ice cream drips down sticky hands,
Laughter echoes across the sands.

Flip-flops dance, a funny sound,
As seagulls squawk around the ground,
A beach ball flies through the air,
Watch out! Clean your hair, beware!

Sips of soda spill in glugs,
While surfers attempt to catch some bugs,
The sunset glows, a wild affair,
With frisbees soaring everywhere!

It's time to toast with coconut shells,
Sirens sing of sandy tales,
As waves crash down, we laugh and cheer,
Cheers to summer, brings us cheer!

The Caress of Sweet Mango

Juicy mango, what a mess,
Sticky fingers, that's the guess!
Peeling skin, what a fun fight,
With fruity battles in the light!

Slurping juice with silly grins,
Spilling some on sister's chin,
A tropical feast we can't resist,
And oh! The taste, it's pure bliss!

We dance around like happy fools,
In our own grove, ignoring rules,
Mango pits fly through the sky,
While giggles echo, oh my, oh my!

Sun-kissed cheeks and laughter bright,
Chasing shadows into the night,
With laughter sweet as summer's balm,
Summer fruits, they keep us calm!

Dance of the Fireflies

Blinking lights like tiny stars,
Fireflies wobble, zooming cars,
With laughter bright, we chase them down,
Feeling light, the world's our crown!

Glowing dots in a starry sea,
As we squeal with wild glee,
A dance party just for bugs,
Who needs snugs when there are shrugs?

We twirl around in joyful spins,
Spill lemonade and laugh at sins,
The night is warm, our hearts take flight,
Fireflies wink, a silly sight!

In this glow, the world seems right,
Chasing sparks till we lose the light,
With giggles and fun, we end our play,
Waiting for another summer day!

Lush Canopies and Moonlight

Under trees where shadows creep,
Laughter bubbles, no time for sleep,
With makeshift forts made out of sticks,
Hiding from mom's silly tricks!

A hammock swings, and kids collide,
On this wild adventure ride,
Swinging high in the leafy breeze,
Watch out now! Avoid the bees!

Moonlight dances on our faces,
As we embark on silly races,
Who can reach the neighbor's gate?
Without a doubt, we're all first-rate!

With giggles loud, our hearts aglow,
The magic of summer steals the show,
There's nothing sweeter than our cheer,
In lush canopies, summer's here!

Echoes of Serene Shores

Sandy toes and silly hats,
Giggling seagulls chase the chats.
Ice cream drips on cheerful plans,
Dance with crabs and clap your hands.

Coconuts sway, they know the score,
Laughter spills from every shore.
Sunburned noses, laughs so loud,
Flip-flops squeak, we're feeling proud.

Bright kites flutter, a paper parade,
Waves crash in, but we won't fade.
Splashing friends, a playful sight,
Chasing sunsets, that's our delight.

Tropical breeze, a cheeky tease,
Sipping punches while we freeze.
Cracking jokes, we're feeling bold,
With every wave, a story told.

Island Echoes and Laughter

Laughter echoes through the palms,
With every breeze, a tale that charms.
Sun hats bob and music plays,
We stumble through the sunny rays.

Mango slices, oh so sweet,
Sticky fingers can't be beat.
In the shade, we gather round,
Chortles mix with waves' cool sound.

Chasing crabs, we plot and scheme,
Nothing can burst our summer dream.
Banana peels slip, oh what fun,
Falling down, but we still run.

Dancing turtles join our crew,
A goofy waddle, just for you.
Flip-flop battles, we're the queens,
At sunset's whim, we live our dreams.

Fragrant Shores of Yum

Grilled pineapple on a stick,
Juggling coconuts, what a trick!
Sipping juices full of cheer,
A fruity feast, come grab a beer.

Giggling gulls in sunlit play,
Scavenging snacks, they take the day.
Lay on towels, let's catch some rays,
Oh, what a life in endless craze!

Sandcastle kings secure their reign,
With jellyfish as their domain.
Pineapple hats wobble with flair,
Who needs a crown when you've got hair?

Ice cream cones, the melting kind,
Chasing shorts, oh what a find!
With every scoop, we laugh aloud,
At fragrant shores, we stand so proud.

Sunkissed Serenades

Sun-kissed skin, a laugh or two,
Sticky sunblock and a view.
Hula-hoops dance in the air,
Caught in giggles, no time for care.

Inflatable flamingos in a line,
Swimming laps, what fun divine!
Sipped with style, a fruity blend,
Lost on islands, we don't pretend.

Water fights, with splashes great,
Every hit, we just can't wait.
Festive hats and sunglasses bright,
Making memories, pure delight.

The sun drips low, our laughter swells,
Under stars, we share our spells.
With every wink and sandy cheer,
In the warm glow, we hold our dear.

Feast of the Flora

In the garden, blooms so bright,
Bumblebees dance in delight.
Sneaky sunflowers nod with glee,
While pollen floats like confetti.

Little ants form a parade,
Trading crumbs for lemonade.
A dandelion whispers 'cheers!'
As tomatoes burst with laughter, peers.

Mango trees with limbs so wide,
Joke about the fruit inside.
Bananas slip on oozy tunes,
As they groove beneath the moons.

Bright hibiscus share their tales,
Of mischief under rain-filled sails.
Coconuts chime in the breeze,
While limes giggle with such ease.

Joy in Juicy Delights

Watermelons wear a grin,
Juices splash, let the fun begin!
Pineapple dons a polka dot hat,
While grapefruits chat—imagine that!

Silly berries burst with song,
In a fruit bowl, all belong.
Peaches wink, and pomegranates tease,
As nectarines giggle in the trees.

Coconuts roll on sandy shores,
Fighting over the best whoores.
Mangoes jump into a spree,
Organizing a fruitéd jubilee!

Kiwi giggles, feeling spry,
While cherries make a pie up high.
Each slice shared with friends so true,
In this juicy slice of summer's queue.

Mirage of Monsoon Magic

Raindrops tap on leafy roofs,
Silly frogs wear raincoat hooves.
Clouds are cotton candy fluff,
As creatures sing, 'We're never tough!'

Mud puddles sprout tiny boats,
Ducklings race with squeaky coats.
A rainbow's peeking through the mist,
While light shows off, it can't resist.

The spiders spin in quirky threads,
Making hats, and fun your heads!
As lightning plays with flashes bright,
The thunder laughs, 'This feels just right!'

Dancing drops upon my nose,
Nature's tickle, heaven knows.
With every splash, we feel alive,
In this magic where we thrive.

Secrets of the Summer Jungle

In the jungle, secrets hide,
Parrots squawk, they can't abide.
Monkeys swing from vine to vine,
Dropping fruits, oh how divine!

Sloths just chuckle, moving slow,
While jaguars strike a pose, a show.
A snake whispers, 'Don't tell a soul,'
As crickets croon the evening's roll.

Lemurs laugh and share a snack,
As hippos take a joyride back.
Each tree tells tales of days gone by,
Where every critter passes by.

Jungle parties never cease,
Amidst the chaos, find your peace.
From fireflies to the bright moonlight,
Summer secrets bloom, oh what a sight!

Lush Hues of Paradise

The sun spilled juice on the grass,
Monkey stole my drink, oh alas!
Bananas laughing in the trees,
While a toucan giggles at the bees.

Bright flip-flops in a sandy race,
With crabs showing off their pace.
Bikinis blush in tropical glow,
As sunscreen flies, oh what a show!

Pineapple hats bobbing in fun,
The whole beach party's just begun!
Seagulls squawk with a cheeky twist,
As I try to catch the summer mist.

But watch your drink, here comes the tide,
It's either that or a crab that slides.
We'll laugh it off with fruity cheer,
In this paradise, summer's near!

Dancing Waves and Distant Horizons

Waves are wiggling on the shore,
While surfers tumble, what a chore!
Sunburned noses, a funny sight,
As beach balls take to dizzy flight.

Children's giggles clash with the foam,
Splashing parents far from home.
Seashells trade secrets, have a chat,
While a crab thinks he's a diplomat!

Kites are soaring, colors collide,
As jellyfish swim with deride.
A funny fish with googly eyes,
Hiding behind a wave, oh what a disguise!

A conga line of toes in sand,
I trip and fall, how unplanned!
Each wave is a dance, wild and free,
In this summer's funny jubilee!

Coconut Caress

Coconuts rolling, a cheeky spree,
I look up, it's falling on me!
They laugh from the tree, such glee,
While I dodge and weave with pure esprit.

The rum punch spills on my new shirt,
A taste explosion, sweet and flirt.
Let's twirl and swirl on this sunlit dance,
As pineapples twirl in a fruit romance!

Sipping on breezes, feeling so spry,
Until a seagull drops by, oh my!
He eyes my snack, with a bold request,
"Give me some, you're really blessed!"

Yet we share laughs and sticky hands,
As we paint smiles in the sands.
In this land where coconuts tease,
Life's just one long, sweet, crazy breeze!

Vibrant Nights and Starry Skies

Under twinkling stars, we gather tight,
Salsa dancing under pale moonlight.
Laughter echoes with every twist,
As the DJ spins, none can resist!

A parrot squawks inappropriate jokes,
While fireflies prance in neon cloaks.
Hula hoops whirl, and I trip once more,
As my friends cheer, wanting to roar!

Feasting on tacos, with guac so divine,
But watch for the salsa; it might make you whine!
The sun sets low, a pineapple pie,
While I'm juggling fruit, oh my, oh my!

We toast with laughter, our cups held high,
"To vibrant nights and stars up in the sky!"
With goofy grins and toes in the sand,
Every moment shared is truly grand!

Beneath the Golden Horizon

Sunburned noses and sandy toes,
Lemons and limes in fruity prose.
Cocktails spill like laughter shared,
Seagulls swoop like they just dared.

Flip-flops squeak, they roam about,
Dancing to tunes, without a doubt.
Coconuts rolling on the floor,
Who's bringing snacks? We need some more!

Jellyfish jokes, oh what a sight,
Watch the waves dance with delight.
Crabs in suits, they strut with pride,
At the beach, we all collide.

As the sun dips, we swap tall tales,
Of runaway boats and mysterious sails.
A sunburned lobster, that's the score,
We'll laugh till our cheeks go sore.

The Edge of Paradise

Palm trees swaying, doing the twist,
Join the conga line, you can't resist!
Flip-flops flapping, it's a crazy show,
Can't tell if that's a dancer or a coconut's blow.

Mangoes dribble down your chin,
As we feast like kings, let the fun begin!
Sunglasses on, our shades are bright,
It's a party here, every single night.

A parrot squawks, "Who looks like a fool?"
As we dance in sand, making our own rules.
Laughter erupts, it's a tropical spree,
While we look for a chair—oh, that's a bee!

Sunsets blaze with orange and pink,
Time for ice cream, we can't even think.
With laughter that echoes, we toast to the sun,
On the edge of paradise, life's just begun.

Drift Away in the Tropics

Floating on floats with an accidental splash,
We giggle and tumble, it's quite the crash.
The sun's a smile resting so high,
As we dive for treasure, oh my, oh my!

Pool noodles bobbing like boats on the sea,
"Not it!" we shout, as we dodge with glee.
Ice cream meltdowns, sticky and bright,
Chasing the dog as he bolts in fright.

Snorkels around our necks like bad bling,
We chase fish that swim and giggle and sing.
Who found the seashell? It's all a bluff,
Hiding behind laughter, is that enough?

As the stars twinkle, we dance in the night,
All pretenses gone, it feels just right.
In the warm night air, every moment's a cheer,
Drifting away, it's the best time of year.

Breezy Bliss

A breeze blows softly, hints of coconuts,
Waves crash gently, "Hey, don't get in ruts!"
Sunglasses on, we strike silly poses,
Matching our drinks with the cute pink roses.

Locals laugh as we try to fit in,
Salsa dancing, oh where to begin?
The piñata swings, but who's holding the stick?
A candy explosion, it happened so quick!

Parrots on shoulders, make for a show,
Giving us makeup tips—oh no, oh no!
Under the palms, we giggle and sway,
With breezy bliss, we plan our next play.

As the sun sets low, the stars come to greet,
We roast marshmallows and dance to the beat.
In silly sombreros, we just can't resist,
This breezy adventure is one for the list.

Coral Reefs and Dreams Afloat

Beneath the waves, the fishes twirl,
A clownfish jokes, gives bubbles a whirl.
Corals wear hats, all colors bright,
They dance in the sun, oh what a sight!

Starfish debate, who can sit still,
While crabs do the cha-cha, it's quite the thrill.
A sea turtle groans, just wants a nap,
As dolphins show off their newest cap.

Seahorses giggle in twinkling tides,
While jellyfish float on their jelly ride.
With every splash, the ocean's a play,
In this underwater cabaret!

So grab your snorkel, come join the cheer,
In coral reefs' laughter, there's nothing to fear!
From flipping fish to the sun's warm glee,
Summer fun swims in the deep blue sea!

Rhythm of the Rainforest

In the jungle, outside my shack,
Monkeys swing, never look back.
A toucan's beak, pure rainbow delight,
But watch out for frogs, they hop in the night!

Parrots gossip while perched on high,
Sipping raindrops, sharing a fry.
The sloths take their sweet time to move,
In this leafy groove, all find their groove.

A jaguar sneezes, oh what a sound!
And every creature jumps all around.
With a beat from the trees and a hum from the ants,
The rhythm of life gives all a chance.

So join the chorus, it's nature's jam,
With giggles and grumbles, it's all a glam.
In the rainforest, where laughter is free,
The punchline's in every coconut tree!

Papaya Whispers

Underneath the papaya's shade,
The fruits gossip about the parade.
A lizard in shades brags with flair,
While the honeybees dance without a care!

Smooth ripe papayas, so sweet and round,
They pop jokes as they tumble down.
"Did you hear about the mango's plight?"
"Oh please," they chuckle, "it's quite a sight!"

Squirrels hoard rinds, they're in on the fun,
Juggling their treasures, they're second to none.
With whispers of fruit and a laugh in the air,
Papaya tales ripple everywhere.

So slice a piece, get a taste of cheer,
A fruity buffet, summer's premiere!
In this orchard of giggles, let's all stay,
In papaya's embrace, it's the silliest way!

Tropical Twilight Revelations

At dusk, the sun yawns, paints skies with gold,
   Crickets chirp secrets, their tales unfold.
   Flamingos gather, flipping their wings,
   In the tropical haze, like they're kings!

The coconut drinks, oh what a tease,
Under palm trees swaying in the breeze.
A turtle wears shades, looking quite suave,
As fireflies buzz with a glow that'll rave.

The night blooms with laughter, stars join the spree,
   As frogs croak their songs, inviting you and me.
   A party of critters, they dance and they sway,
   In twilight's embrace, let's laugh and play!

So grab a friend, let the night take flight,
   In the heart of the tropics, everything's right.
With joy and delight where the wild creatures roam,
   In this twilight of fun, we all find our home!

Juicy Moments Under the Sun

Mangoes swing from trees so high,
With giggles flying up to the sky.
Pineapples wear their crowns with pride,
As we all dance, the juice our guide.

Lemons roll away, slippery and bold,
While we chase them, being young and old.
Coconuts wave, say bye to the ground,
Creating laughter, a joy so profound.

Lullabies by the Lagoon

The waves hum tunes, soft and light,
While crabs tap dance, oh what a sight!
Fish in bowties swim by fast,
They giggle and splash, a merry cast.

Sunsets blush, the sky's a clown,
As beach balls tumble and fall down.
Sandcastles lean, seeking their fate,
A royal parade of shells, first-rate!

Serenade of Sunsets

The sun dips low, a showtime grand,
Seagulls squawk, on a musical band.
Bikinis flutter like flags on parade,
While flip-flops stumble, a grand charade.

Ice cream cones melt in sticky hands,
As we laugh at our sandy strands.
Sunburns add a crimson flair,
While humor swims sun-kissed in the air.

Dreaming Under the Palms

Palms sway gently, a ticklish tease,
Their coconuts drop with the slightest breeze.
We set up camp for a hammock nap,
Only to find a squirrel's funny cap!

The breeze whispers secrets, in giggles they share,
While chubby lizards bask without a care.
Bugs do the cha-cha on our picnic spread,
While we laugh till we fall, half asleep in our bed.

Wilderness of Watermelon

In a jungle of green, where fruit takes the stage,
A watermelon smiles, looking quite sage.
It wobbles and giggles, a huge, juicy ball,
Waiting for summer's sweet festival call.

The squirrels throw a party, the birds grab a slice,
They dance with the breeze, oh, isn't it nice?
With seeds like confetti, they launch in the air,
As rinds pile high, covers the grassy square.

A picnic unfolds, and all join the feast,
But don't let the ants come; they'll munch like a beast!
With juice dripping down, it's a colorful sight,
Laughs echo around, hearts feel light as a kite.

So grab that big berry, don't let it roll free,
In this wilderness fun, come swing in with glee.
They'll holler and yell, who can eat the most?
In summer's wild land, we'll celebrate and boast.

Sweet Currents of the Coast

On the sandy shores, where the sun loves to play,
Sea turtles and crabs join in a ballet.
With flip-flops a-floppin', the waves start to cheer,
As beach balls are tossed to the rhythm so clear.

A seagull swoops down, with snacks on the side,
Chasing kids' laughter, oh what a ride!
Sandcastles built tall, but the tide loves to tease,
One wave wipes them out, like a sneeze in the breeze.

Ice-cream cones melting, a sticky delight,
A kid's joyful shriek turns the chaos to light.
With laughter and splashes, the sun starts to hide,
The ocean waves whisper, come take a wild ride!

So gather your friends, let the fun never cease,
In sweet currents of joy, find your summer peace.
Let the tide take you high, with giggles galore,
'Til the sun makes you sleepy, and you dream about more.

A Mosaic of Melodies

In the heart of the grove, where the fruit bats hang,
A chorus of colors begins with a clang.
Bananas are laughing, coconuts sway,
While parrots squawk out their bright serenade.

Guitars made of leaves strum a tune so divine,
While mangoes keep dancing, all sweet and on-time.
The breeze joins the band, giving rhythm and rhyme,
A mosaic of melodies, splashed bold in the prime.

The turtles all tap, like they know every step,
While fireflies twinkle, making shadows adept.
With guava Smiles painted, we dance through the night,
In this symphony lush, our worries take flight.

So grab a peach pair, swing into the beat,
Let laughter and fun lift you off of your feet.
In a tropical groove, where joy never fades,
Join in on the magic that summer parades.

Nectar of the Tropics

With a splash and a slurp, sip the juice of delight,
A fruit punch explosion, party starts every night.
Pineapples frolic, with each twist and a twirl,
In this nectar-filled land, comes summer's sweet whirl.

The lizards all dance, wearing sunglasses so cool,
As waves crash on rocks, like a beach party pool.
With nectar like candy, the bees buzz around,
Turning our laughter to pure nectar sound.

Papayas wear hats made of palm frond and cheer,
While mangoes get jazzy, bringing grooves to the sphere.
The rhythm is sticky, the sweetness insane,
In a world full of fruit, who could stand the mundane?

So sip your delight, let that laughter abound,
In this nectar party, joy truly is found.
With fruit as our treasure, and sun shining bright,
We'll dance through the tropics, till day turns to night.

www.ingramcontent.com/pod-product-compliance
Lightning Source LLC
Chambersburg PA
CBHW072222070526
44585CB00015B/1447